THIS GIRAFFE BOOK BELONGS TO:

_____

_____

_____

_____

ONE CHILD ONE SEED

A SOUTH AFRICAN COUNTING BOOK

GIRAFFE BOOKS

For Isis and Makeda – K.C.

First published 2002 by Frances Lincoln Limited
One Child One Seed copyright © Frances Lincoln Limited 2002

First published in 2001 by Pan Macmillan South Africa.
This ONE CHILD ONE SEED edition published in 2004 by Giraffe Books, an imprint of
Pan Macmillan South Africa.
PO Box 411717, Craighall, 2024, Johannesburg
www.panmacmillan.co.za

Text copyright © Kathryn Cave 2002
Photographs copyright © Oxfam Activities Limited and Gisèle Wulfsohn 2002

ISBN 0-620280-88-3

Printed by Pinetown Printers
2004

Oxfam and the publishers would like to thank Nothando and her family, their community in Nkandla district,
KwaZulu Natal and Kwazi Mazibuko for their enthusiastic support.

Oxfam believes every human being is entitled to a life of dignity and opportunity. Working with others we
use our ingenuity, knowledge and wealth of experience to make resources and money work harder.
From practical work with individuals through to influencing world policy we aim to enable the world's
poorest people to create a future that no longer needs Oxfam.

ONE CHILD ONE SEED

A SOUTH AFRICAN COUNTING BOOK

Kathryn Cave • *Photographs by* Gisèle Wulfsohn

In Association with Oxfam

PAN MACMILLAN SA

 One child, one seed.

Nothando lives with her Aunt Nomusa (in red) and her Grandmother Betty (in blue). Her big sister and her mother are on the right of the picture, and her brother is on the left. They live nearby and spend a lot of time with Nothando.

Here is Nothando with her pumpkin seed. She lives in South Africa, where pumpkins grow all summer long.

 **TWO** hands to plant the seed.

The homestead where Nothando lives is in a district called Nkandla. The main house has a kitchen, a living room and a bedroom.

Its walls (shown in the picture) are made of wood, mud and grass. They are then plastered and painted. The roof is corrugated iron. Outside there are three thatched huts called rondavels, used for cooking and storage.

Nothando buries the pumpkin seed in the earth. It's November, the beginning of summer. The summer rains will help the seed to grow. By February, it will have grown into a pumpkin big enough to eat.

 **Three** ways to help it grow.

Some years the summer rains are very heavy, and the river that flows through Nkandla floods. Too much water is bad for the crops: they rot, and when the water finally drains away there's lots of clearing up to do. Women do the work by hand, with help from the children.

Nothando's brother Siphelele has a spade to dig up weeds. Their friend Nobuhle has water in her bucket to keep the little plant alive in dry weather. Nothando helps with the hoe.

 Four creatures watch.

All the animals on the homestead have to earn their keep. Cows do that by giving milk and meat. Chicks provide eggs and meat once they're fully grown. Cats and dogs make themselves useful by chasing and catching rats.

If these cows get too close they'll tread on the little pumpkin plant, or even eat it.

Who will see that they don't? Nothando's cousin Mongezi gets that job. He's the family cowherd.

 **5** Five friends to pick the pumpkin.

Any month can be harvest time because vegetables grow all year round. Out in the fields and in the vegetable garden you can find cabbage, spinach, beetroot, potatoes, beans and mealies (the local name for maize).

The pumpkin's stalk has dried out. That means the pumpkin's ripe. It's time for Nothando and her friends to pick it and carry it home.

 **Six** things to buy.

Sibongile store is a ten-minute walk from the homestead. The town of Nkandla is much further, and there aren't many shops there – just a few that sell food or clothes. There's a farmers' market in the town, too.

Now it's time to turn the pumpkin into a feast! Nothando walks to the store to stock up with sugar, mealie meal, bread and margarine, and a passionfruit drink.
The curry powder is for a vegetable curry, tomorrow.

Seven weary walkers.

It's a long walk home for dinner after an afternoon in the vegetable garden. But that's the way most people get around here: on foot.

The roads around Nkandla are just dirt, and in the rainy season they can't be used. When it's not too wet, this small van runs a taxi service three times a day from outside Nothando's school into town and back again. The half-hour trip costs 6 rand each way.

The nearest big city is Durban, 300 km away. Nothando dreams of going there one day.

 **Eight** slices of ripe pumpkin.

Tonight Aunt Nomusa is chief cook. First she cuts off the pumpkin's tough peel. Then she scrapes out the seeds, and cuts the pumpkin into slices. It looks a lot smaller now – let's hope there's enough to go round.

Aunt Nomusa adds mealie meal to the cooked pumpkin to thicken it, and sugar to make it sweet. The homestead has no fridge, so fresh food has to be cooked and eaten before it goes bad.

Many families can't afford to cook more than once a day, usually in the evening. Those who can, cook lunch or a midday snack too: bean soup or chicken and mealie meal. Breakfast is usually a mug of tea and some bread.

23

9 **Nine** hungry eaters waiting for a trea[t]

Games make the time until dinner pass more quickly. This is Am I In?, Nothando's favourite. You mark out squares on the ground, and hop round kicking a stone from square to square. If the stone misses the right square, you're out.

Most of the games here use objects that cost nothing, like sticks and stones.

Nomusa is cooking a big pot of a traditional Zulu dish: 'isijingi'. Tonight the weather's hot, so she prepares the meal outside. Everyone stops to watch.

 **Ten** dinner plates piled high.

It's dinner time at last. And there's plenty for everyone!

When the meal is over, the children clear away. They wash up under the cold tap beside the house, scrubbing the plates with their hands or a wet cloth until they are clean again.

The isijingi's gone now, every bit. There's just one part of the pumpkin left. Can you guess what it is?

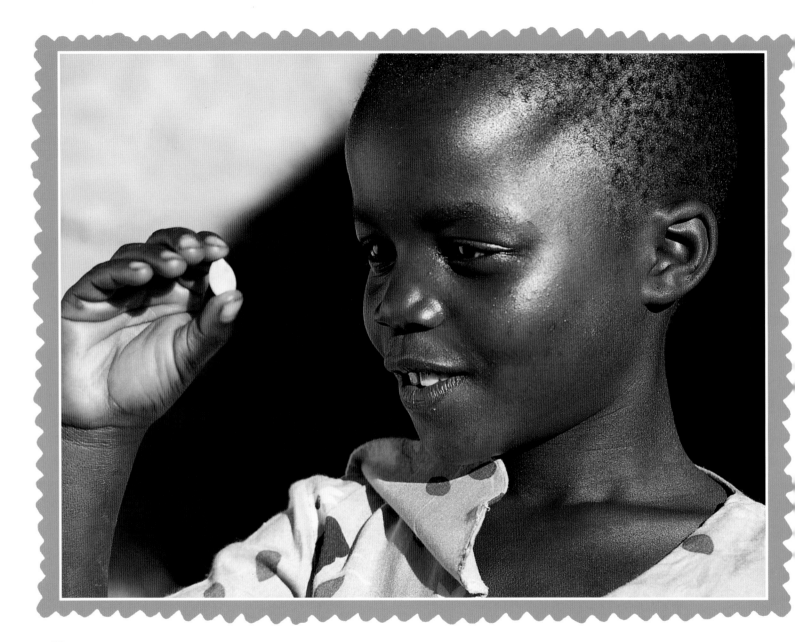

 **One** child, one seed to plant next time.

1   one

2   two

3   three

4   four

5   five

6   six

7   seven

8   eight

9   nine

10 ten